Queen Cohen, Petitioner, v. Public Housing Administration et al. U.S. Supreme Court Transcript of Record with Supporting Pleadings

THURGOOD MARSHALL, SHELBY MYRICK, J LEE RANKIN

Queen Cohen, Petitioner, v. Public Housing Administration et al.
Petition / THURGOOD MARSHALL / 1958 / 505 / 358 U.S. 928 / 79 S.Ct. 315 / 3 L.Ed.2d 302 / 11-8-1958
Queen Cohen, Petitioner, v. Public Housing Administration et al.
Brief in Opposition (P) / SHELBY MYRICK / 1958 / 505 / 358 U.S. 928 / 79 S.Ct. 315 / 3 L.Ed.2d 302 / 12-6-1958
Queen Cohen, Petitioner, v. Public Housing Administration et al.
Brief in Opposition (P) / J LEE RANKIN / 1958 / 505 / 358 U.S. 928 / 79 S.Ct. 315 / 3 L.Ed.2d 302 / 12-10-1958

Queen Cohen, Petitioner, v. Public Housing
Administration et al. U.S. Supreme Court
Transcript of Record with Supporting Pleadings

Table of Contents

IN THE

Supreme Court of the United States

October Term 1958

No. 505 524

QUEEN COHEN,

Petitioner,

—v.—

PUBLIC HOUSING ADMINISTRATION, *et al.,*

Respondents.

PETITION FOR WRIT OF CERTIORARI TO THE UNITED STATES COURT OF APPEALS FOR THE FIFTH CIRCUIT

THURGOOD MARSHALL
CONSTANCE BAKER MOTLEY
10 Columbus Circle
New York 19, N. Y.

A. T. WALDEN
28 Butler Street, N. E.
Atlanta 3, Georgia

Attorneys for Petitioner

LAWYERS PRESS, INC., 214 William St., N. Y. C. 38; 'Phone: BEekman 3-2300

SUBJECT INDEX

TABLE OF CASES

STATUTES:

OTHER AUTHORITIES:

Supreme Court of the United States

October Term 1958

No. ....

❖

QUEEN COHEN,

Petitioner,

—v.—

PUBLIC HOUSING ADMINISTRATION, *et al.,*

Respondents.

❖

PETITION FOR WRIT OF CERTIORARI TO THE UNITED STATES COURT OF APPEALS FOR THE FIFTH CIRCUIT

Petitioner prays that a Writ of Certiorari issue to review the judgment of the United States Court of Appeals for the Fifth Circuit.

Opinions Below

The opinion of the United States Court of Appeals for the Fifth Circuit is reported. *Cohen* v. *Public Housing Administration, et al.,* 257 F. 2d 73 (1958). The opinion of the United States District Court for the Southern District of Georgia, Savannah Division, is also reported. *Heyward, et al.* v. *Public Housing Administration, et al.,* 154 F. Supp. 589 (1957). Copies of these decisions are set forth in Appendix A and the printed record.

Jurisdiction

The jurisdiction of this Court is invoked pursuant to the provisions of Title 28, United States Code, §1254(1).

The opinion of the United States Court of Appeals for the Fifth Circuit was rendered on June 30th, 1958. Petition for rehearing was denied on August 11, 1958.

Questions Presented

1. Whether a plaintiff qualified for admission to federally-aided public housing lacks standing to sue to enjoin the policy of limiting certain projects to white and others to Negro occupancy, which derives from local application of the Public Housing Administration's racial equity requirement, simply because the court, weighing disputed testimony, found that she failed to prove formal application to and express exclusion from a particular project?

2. Whether there is any constitutional and/or statutory duty on the Public Housing Administration to refrain from approving and aiding racially segregated public housing projects, and to require that federally-aided public housing be made available on a non-discriminatory basis in accordance with the statutory preferences for admission?

Constitutional And Statutory Provisions Involved

This case involves the due process clause of the Fifth Amendment to the Constitution of the United States and the due process and equal protection clauses of the Fourteenth Amendment thereto.

In addition, the following sections of Title 42, United States Code are involved: 1402(1), (14); 1410(g); 1415(8) (a), (b) and (c); 1982; 1983.

Also involved is the Public Housing Administration's regulation requiring racial equity. These statutory provisions and this regulation are set forth in Appendix B.

Statement Of The Case

This suit was originally brought in the United States District Court for the District of Columbia by the filing of a complaint against the Public Housing Administration in September 1952 in an attempt to enjoin the expenditure of federal funds for the construction of a project on a Negro residential site which would be limited to white occupancy. The district court dismissed the suit on its merits on the ground that separate and equal facilities were being provided for Negroes. *Heyward, et al.* v. *Housing and Home Finance Agency, et al.*, Civil Action No. 3991-52 unreported (copy of opinion of May 8, 1953 set forth in Appendix C).

On appeal to the United States Court of Appeals for the District of Columbia Circuit the dismissal was affirmed on the ground that the Housing Authority of Savannah, Georgia was a conditionally necessary party and plaintiffs should therefore bring the suit where both parties could be brought before the court. *Heyward, et al.* v. *Public Housing Administration*, 214 F. 2d 222 (1954).

Suit was thereafter filed in May 1954 in the United States District Court for the Southern District of Georgia, Savannah Division, against the Public Housing Administration (PHA), its Atlanta Field Office Director, the Housing Authority of Savannah, Georgia (SHA), its members and executive director. Jurisdiction was invoked pursuant to Title 28, United States Code, §§1331 and 1343(3) (R. 2-3). The district court dismissed the complaint on SHA's motion to dismiss and PHA's motion for summary judgment on the ground that separate but equal facilities was still the law applicable to this case and on the ground that PHA is not involved in the controversy. *Heyward, et al.* v. *Public Housing Administration, et al.*, 135 F. Supp. 217 (1955).

An appeal was taken from this judgment to the court below where it was reversed in part and affirmed in part. *Heyward, et al.* v. *Public Housing Administration, et al.*, (5th Cir. 1956) 238 F. 2d 689. Affirmance related only to dismissal of the complaint as to the Atlanta Field Office Director of PHA. In reversing, the court held that the complaint stated a cause of action within the provisions of Title 42, United States Code, §1983 and sufficiently alleged jurisdiction over PHA under Title 28, United States Code, §1331.

After a full trial on the merits, the district court dismissed petitioner's case on the ground that the evidence failed to establish that she had made application for admission to any project and the undisputed testimony shows that she was not entitled to a statutory preference for admission. Title 42, United States Code, §1410(g) or 1415 (8)(c). *Heyward, et al.* v. *Public Housing Administration, et al.*, 154 F. Supp. 589 (1957).

Upon the second appeal to the court below it affirmed dismissal on the ground that since petitioner did not make application, she has no standing to sue. It ruled that 1) the district court's pertinent finding that petitioner did not make application does not appear to be clearly erroneous as required for reversal by Rule 52(a), Federal Rules of Civil Procedure, 28 U. S. C. A.; 2) in the absence of any attempt to apply, there is no reasonably certain proof that petitioner actually desired in some earlier year to become a tenant in Fred Wessels Homes; 3) an application by petitioner would not have been a vain act or the yielding to an unconstitutional demand.

However, the court below then held in the alternative that since this case involves voluntary segregation, such segregation is not subject to constitutional attack. It ruled that both the pleadings and the proof denied segregation. It noted testimony of the executive director of SHA to the effect that "in his opinion actual segregation is essential to the success of a program of public housing in Savannah" and ruled that,

> "If the people involved think that such is the case and if Negroes and whites desire to maintain voluntary segregation for their common good, there is certainly no law to prevent such cooperation. Neither the Fifth nor the Fourteenth Amendments operates positively to command integration of the races, but only negatively to forbid governmentally enforced segregation."

Cohen v. *Public Housing Administration, et al.,* 257 F. 2d 73, 78 (1958).

This decision was based upon the following facts appearing in the record:

1. The housing program involved in this case is low rent public housing provided for by the United States Housing Act of 1937, as amended.[1] This is a program whereby the federal government, through PHA, and local public housing agencies established by law in the several states, enter into contracts for the construction, operation and maintenance of decent, safe and sanitary dwellings. These dwellings are available to only those families who, because of their low incomes, are unable to secure decent, safe and sanitary private housing at the lowest rates at which such private housing is being provided in the locality (R. 85). PHA and SHA have entered into contracts for construction, operation and maintenance of nine such public housing projects in the City of Savannah (R. 81).

---

[1] Title 42, United States Code, §1401, *et seq.*

2. The record in this case discloses that petitioner meets the income requirements for admission which have been established by SHA and approved by PHA.[2] (R. 133, 206. See Plaintiff's Exhibit 10, Answer to Interrogatory No. 6.)

3. Petitioner was displaced from her home when a commercial enterprise which had been located on the site of Fred Wessels Homes moved its business across the street to the site of petitioner's former residence (R. 204-205). When petitioner received a thirty-day notice from her landlord to vacate, she went to the office of SHA which is located in the Fred Wessels Homes, for the purpose of making application for a family unit (R. 131).[3] She was advised that the Fred Wessels project was not for Negro families (R. 133). She was not given a formal application blank. She was told to apply at Fellwood Homes, a Negro project (R. 133). At that time the buildings were completed but unoccupied (R. 135). Appellant desires to live in Fred Wessels Homes (R. 139). She is the mother of four children, one of whom is in the armed services of the United States (R. 133).[4] Her husband is employed and earns fifty dollars per week (R. 206).

4. The Director-Secretary of SHA insisted that petitioner and other Negroes never applied for admission to Fred Wessels Homes. Upon the trial he was asked, "Q. If a negro applied for admission to the Fred Wessels Homes

---

[2] Title 42, United States Code, §§1402(1), 1415(8)(a).

[3] Families having the greatest urgency of need are given preference for admission by virtue of the provisions of Title 42, United States Code, §1415(8)(c). See also Title 42, United States Code, §1415(8)(b).

[4] Families of servicemen have preference. Title 42, United States Code, §1410(g). See Annual Contributions Contract, Part II, Sections 206, 208, 209, Plaintiff's Exhibit 1. PHA has the responsibility for seeing that the preferences are applied (R. 175).

would you put him in there? Is that what you are saying? A. No. He would be given consideration, but I don't know what I would do. . . . Q. Are you saying you would admit negroes? A. I didn't say that." (R. 127)

5. The evidence shows that other Negroes also went into the office located in Fred Wessels Homes to apply for housing. Those who did so were assigned to Fellwood Homes. None was considered for admission or assigned to Fred Wessels Homes (R. 95-97).

6. Prior to the opening of Fred Wessels Homes for occupancy, SHA publicly announced that this project would be for white occupancy (R. 112).

7. There is no central tenant application office in Savannah. Applicants generally apply at the particular projects they desire to enter (R. 82). However, the ultimate determination as to the project in which the applicant family will reside remains with SHA (R. 96-97).

8. Limitation of certain projects to Negro occupancy and the limitation of others to white occupancy is approved by PHA through approval of SHA's Development Programs which must reflect application of PHA's racial equity requirement (R. 54-55).[5] PHA, by its administrative rules and regulations, requires that a local program "reflect equitable provision for eligible families of all races determined on the approximate volume of their respective needs for such housing" (Plaintiff's Exhibit 2, PHA Racial Policy). The need of the two races is determined primarily by the approximate volume of substandard housing occupied by each race (R. 91-92). Application of this formula re-

---

[5] The two most recent Development Programs were sent up to this Court in their original form. Plaintiff's Exhibits 7 and 8. These programs designate the racial occupancy of each project.

sulted in the present determination that equitable provision for Negro families in Savannah requires that they be provided with approximately 75% of the total number of family units and that equitable provision for white families requires that they be provided with approximately 25% of the total number of family units (R. 106-107). However, Negroes presently occupy only 42.7% of the existing units and whites, because of the addition of the two former PHA owned defense housing projects to the public housing supply, presently occupy 57.3% of the existing units (R. 104). The Development Programs, when approved by PHA, become a part of the contracts between PHA and SHA (R. 178).

9. Once a determination is made as to the approximate per cent of the total number of units to be occupied by Negro and white families, PHA would object to a deviation from these percentages by SHA (R. 181). The Director-Secretary of SHA viewed the admission of Negroes to Fred Wessels Homes as resulting in a violation of PHA's racial equity requirement (R. 121-122).

10. The most recently completed project in Savannah is Fred Wessels Homes which opened for occupancy in 1954 (R. 188). This project has been built on a site located approximately seven blocks from the main business area of Savannah (R. 114). It contains 250 family units at a cost of approximately $2,800,000 (R. 113). Prior to construction of this project, the site was occupied by 250 Negro families and 70 white families (R. 102-103). This project has been limited to white occupancy (R. 103).

11. Petitioner did not join this suit as a named plaintiff until action was instituted against both PHA and SHA in Savannah (R. 137-138). When suit was filed in the District of Columbia the action was brought by 13 named plaintiffs

on behalf of themselves and others similarly situated. Fred Wessels Homes had not yet been constructed and the site occupants had not yet been displaced. When suit was re-instituted about two years later in Savannah, after the decision of the Court of Appeals for the District of Columbia, only 4 of the original plaintiffs were named again as plaintiffs. These 4 were joined by 14 new plaintiffs suing on behalf of themselves and others similarly situated (R. 1, 7). By this time, Fred Wessels Homes had opened for white occupancy (R. 188); 250 Negro families, including 15 plaintiffs, had already been displaced and relocated (R. 102-103, 116-118, 126). However, the majority of the displaced Negro families had found housing on their own, had not accepted relocation assistance from SHA and had not accepted segregated Negro public housing (R. 88-89).

12. This case did not come to trial until 3 years after it had been instituted in Savannah. On the trial petitioner was asked over and over again by SHA's counsel why she wanted to live in Fred Wessels Homes and whether she really wanted to live there. Her answers clearly indicate a genuine desire to live there. She has lived in the area all her life (R. 139-140).

Reasons Relied On For Allowance Of Writ

I. The Public Importance Of This Case.

This case reveals that despite decisions of this Court voiding legislative and judicial enforcement of residential racial segregation, *Buchanan* v. *Warley*, 245 U. S. 60; *Shelley* v. *Kraemer*, 334 U. S. 1; *Hurd* v. *Hodge*, 334 U. S. 24; *Barrows* v. *Jackson*, 346 U. S. 249, the executive arm of the federal government, through an agency concerned with the provision of housing, has continued to approve, participate in, and to finance the construction, operation and maintenance of racially segregated housing developments. The Public Housing Administration has not only approved, participated in, and financed racially segregated public housing developments in the southern states but has done so in northern states as well. See e.g. *Detroit Housing Commission* v. *Lewis* (6th Cir. 1955), 226 F. 2d 180; *Housing Authority of City & County of San Francisco* v. *Banks*, 120 Cal. App. 2d 1, 260 P. 2d 668, cert. den. 347 U. S. 974; *Jones* v. *City of Hamtramck* (S. D. Mich. 1954), 121 F. Supp. 123; *Vann* v. *Toledo Metropolitan Housing Authority* (N. D. Ohio 1953), 113 F. Supp. 210.

PHA is only one of several federal housing agencies concerned with the provision of housing. The Federal Housing Administration and the Veterans' Administration are also concerned with the provision of housing through the federal government's mortgage insurance programs. These agencies are likewise involved in the development of racially segregated housing communities. See e.g., *Johnson* v. *Levitt & Sons, Inc.* (E. D. Pa. 1955), 131 F. Supp. 114; *New York State Commission Against Discrimination* v. *Pelham Hall Apartments, Inc.*, 170 N. Y. S. 2d 750 (1958); *Ming* v. *Horgan*, Superior Court, Sacramento County, California, June 23, 1958, No. 97130, 3 Race Relations Law Reporter 693 (1958).

In addition to PHA, FHA and VA, it now appears that the Urban Renewal Administration, the federal government's newest agency concerned with the provision of housing and the renewal of whole cities is now involved in the redevelopment of racially segregated housing communities. See Johnstone, *The Federal Urban Renewal Program*, 25 University of Chicago Law Rev. 301, at 337-341 (1958). See, e.g., *Barnes* v. *City of Gadsden, Alabama* (U. S. D. C. N. D. Ala. 1958), Civ. No. 1091, 3 Race Relations Law Reporter 712 (1958); *Tate* v. *City of Eufaula, Alabama* (U. S.

D. C. M. D. Ala. 1958), Civil Action No. 1442-N, unreported, decided August 6, 1958.

The phenomenal growth and influence of federal agencies concerned with the provision of housing since the early 1930's makes manifest the role of the federal administrator in the housing market.[6] Public housing, mortgaged insured housing, and urban renewal housing, where segregated throughout the United States, is supported by federal funds, powers and credits. Federal administrators have, therefore, become primary agents in the extension of segregated living.

Whether there is any constitutional and/or statutory duty on the Public Housing Administration to refrain from approving, participating in, and financing racially segregated public housing projects and to require that federally-aided public housing be made available on a non-discriminatory basis in accordance with the statutory preferences for admission is an important question of federal law which has not been, but should be, settled by this Court.

When the instant case was before the United States District Court for the District of Columbia, *Heyward, et al.* v. *Housing and Home Finance Agency, et al.* (unreported, Civil No. 3991-52, opinion of May 8, 1953 in Appendix C), that court held that the federal government could provide public facilities on a separate but equal basis.

When an appeal was taken to the Court of Appeals for the District of Columbia, *Heyward et al.* v. *Public Housing Administration,* 214 F. 2d 222 (1954), that court did not rule upon the merits as the district court had but, nevertheless, did point out in its opinion that the PHA had ap-

---

[6] Johnstone, *The Federal Urban Renewal Program*, 25 Univ. of Chicago Law Review. 301 (1958).

proved racial segregation in public housing in Savannah, Georgia.

When suit was then instituted in Savannah against both PHA and SHA, the district court there held that the separate but equal doctrine applied to this case and dismissed the complaint, *Heyward, et al.* v. *Public Housing Administration, et al.*, 135 F. Supp. 217 (1955).

Upon the first appeal to the court below, *Heyward, et al.* v. *Public Housing Administration, et al.*, 238 F. 2d 689 (1956), it ruled that "the complaint sets forth allegations which, if proven, would show a failure on the part of PHA to comply with the . . . statutory tenant selection policy, and this would constitute a violation of plaintiffs' rights to due process under the Fifth Amendment" (at 697). That court also ruled that "at the time this action was filed the regulations of PHA required that any local program for the development of low-rent housing reflect equitable provision for eligible families of all races, *but did not require that housing be made available on a non-segregated or non-discriminatory basis*" (emphasis ours) (at 697). In addition to these rulings, the court said: "While it is true that PHA has not been charged by Congress with the duty of preventing discrimination in the leasing of housing project units, what these plaintiffs are saying in effect is that the federal agency is charged with that duty under the Fifth Amendment, and that that duty should be forced upon PHA by the courts through the medium of injunctive process" (at 696).

II. The Court Below Has Decided This Case In Conflict With Applicable Decisions Of This Court And Applicable Principles Established By Decisions Of This Court.

A. In the court below petitioner assigned as error the district court's finding that she had not applied. She also contended that prior application is not a prerequisite to the maintenance of this suit since her case is, that, although eligible for admission, she is not "permitted to make application for any project limited to white occupancy." *Heyward, et al.* v. *Public Housing Administration, et al.* (5th Cir. 1956), 238 F. 2d 689, 698. Petitioner contends that a policy of segregation says, in effect, that she may not apply for a white project—that she may only apply for, would only be considered for admission to, and would only be assigned to, a Negro project, as occurred in the case of other Negroes who applied at Fred Wessels Homes (R. 95-96). Petitioner contends that since segregation is the announced policy (R. 112) application for admission to a particular white project, prior to reversal of this policy or a court injunction enjoining enforcement of the policy, would be a vain act, and equity does not require the doing of a vain act as a condition of relief. In so contending she relied upon the Fourth Circuit's ruling in *School Board of City of Charlottesville, Va.* v. *Allen* (4th Cir. 1956), 240 F. 2d 59, cert. den. 353 U. S. 910, which was followed by the court below, itself, in *Gibson* v. *Board of Public Instruction of Dade County* (5th Cir. 1957), 246 F. 2d 913. See, also, *Bush* v. *Orleans Parish School Board* (E. D. La. 1956), 138 F. Supp. 337, aff'd (5th Cir. 1957), 242 F. 2d 156, 162, cert. den. 354 U. S. 921 and *County School Board of Arlington County, Va.* v. *Thompson* (4th Cir. 1958), 252 F. 2d 929.

In the *Charlottesville* case the Fourth Circuit ruled:

Defendants argue, in this connection (Pupil Placement Law), that plaintiffs have not shown themselves entitled to injunctive relief because they have not individually applied for admission to any particular school and been denied. The answer is that in view of the announced policy of the respective school boards any such application to a school other than a segregated school maintained for Colored people would have been futile; and equity does not require the doing of a vain thing as a condition of relief (at 63-64).

The court below sought to distinguish the instant case from the *Charlottesville* case and the *Gibson* case on two grounds: 1) in each of those cases the plaintiffs had placed themselves on record as desiring practically the same relief as that sought from the court and 2) in each of the cases relied on by petitioner it was admitted that discriminatory segregation of the races was being enforced by the defendant Board, while, . . . in the present case, in both the pleadings and the proof, governmentally enforced segregation is denied.

If bringing the instant case in 1954 and pressing it over a period of more than four years does not place petitioner on record as desiring to be considered for admission and as desiring to be admitted to public housing without discrimination against her solely because of her race and color, then petitioner submits that she can conceive of no more pointed way of putting herself on record as being opposed to racial segregation in public housing. This Court long ago overruled the contention that a Negro who seeks equal protection of the law must first make a prior demand upon the state for such equal protection and give the state an opportunity to act upon such demand before bringing suit. *Sipuel* v. *Board of Regents*, 332 U. S. 631.

Not only was the court below in error in stating categorically that the pleadings denied segregation but it was likewise in error in stating that the proof failed to establish governmentally enforced segregation. In their answer the defendant SHA denied on the one hand that segregation was being enforced and yet, on the other hand, removed all doubt on this question by the following paragraphs set forth therein:

"(a) The white citizens of the United States and the State of Georgia are protected under the Constitution of the United States in their rights to life, liberty, and the pursuit of happiness. To compel the white race to live with, affiliate with, and integrate with the Negro race in their private lives contrary to their wishes, desires, beliefs, customs and traditions, is a denial of their rights under the Fourteenth Amendment to the Constitution of the United States and an invasion of their right to privacy. The right of white tenants of Fred Wessels Homes and other projects of the Housing Authority not to be compelled to live with or among the Negro race, and not to affiliate and integrate with them is a valuable and inalienable right, and the violation of these rights will cause them great mental, psychological and physical distress, injury and hurt. The destruction and abrogation of these rights is a violation of both the Fifth and Fourteenth Amendments to the Constitution and laws of the United States (R. 28).

(b) The policy of separating the white from the colored race in the public housing projects, adopted by the Housing Authority of Savannah, is not based solely because of the fact that the colored race are Negroes, but is largely done in order to preserve the peace and good order of the community. The State of Georgia and the City of Savannah, Georgia, each has a paramount duty under the police power to so regulate its citizens as to prevent disorder and violence, and to preserve the peace, good order and dignity of the community. Furthermore, the separation of the races—that is, the white people from the Negroes by the Housing Authority of Savannah is based largely on the local situation with reference to the residences of the white people and the Negroes in Savannah. The Negroes are assigned to houses located in districts in which they live and which are predominantly occupied by Negroes, and the white people are assigned to units of projects located in the districts where white people predominantly reside.[7] The policy of the Housing Authority of Savannah is now and has been to treat the white race and the colored race separately but equally,—that is to say to afford each equal but separate facilities (R. 28-29).

(c) Experience has shown that the indiscriminate mixing of the white and colored races,—that is to say, white people and Negroes in residential districts leads to frequent and violent disturbances and riots, and such policy leads to a great disturbance of the peace, the good order and tranquility of the community, and often results in violence and riots; and for this reason the separation of the races—that is to say—the white people from the Negroes in residential units erected or to be erected by the Housing Authority of Savannah, is required and is necessary (R. 29).

(d) The white tenants of Fred Wessels Homes and other projects of the Housing Authority of Savannah have a valuable property right and interest in the housing units they occupy in the several projects and in the written leases therefor with the Housing Authority of Savannah, and these valuable property rights are protected by the Due Process of Law Clause of the Fifth Amendment to the Constitution of the United

---

[7] It should be noted that the record clearly discloses that the site on which the white Fred Wessels Homes project was erected was occupied by 250 Negro families and 70 white families (R. 102-103).

States which provides that no property of a citizen shall be taken or destroyed except under due process of law. The occupancy by Negroes of units in these projects assigned to and occupied by white tenants will immediately destroy and take away the valuable property rights of the white tenants in their respective units, and this without their ever having their day in Court" (R. 30).

As for the proof in this case, the record is clear that a policy of racial segregation is being enforced not only by the state agency but by the federal agency also (R. 121-122, 181). As a matter of fact, the court below, in its own opinion, points out that "Mr. Stillwell's testimony has been noted (footnote 7, *supra*) to the effect that in his opinion actual segregation is essential to the success of a program of public housing in Savannah."[8] But even more important is the fact that the federal agency representative who testified finally conceded that PHA would object if the SHA departed from PHA's racial equity requirement (R. 181) application of which results in the limitation of certain units to white and other units to Negro occupancy (R. 106-107).

As pointed out by the Fourth Circuit in the *Thompson* case, *supra,* which was a companion case with the *Charlottesville* case at 240 F. 2d 59, the theory of the segregation cases is often misunderstood. A plaintiff sues to enjoin the segregation policy, not for admission to a particular public facility. Assignment to a particular public facility is left to the public agency involved. If injunction enjoining the policy is disobeyed, only then may admission to a specific facility be ordered. *Brown* v. *Board of Education of Topeka,* 349 U. S. 294.

[8] Mr. Stillwell is the Director-Secretary of the Savannah Housing Authority.

B. After making invalid distinctions between the *Char-lottesville* and other cases cited above, the court below held alternatively that since this case involves voluntary segregation, the proof failing to establish governmentally enforced segregation, such segregation is not constitutionally vulnerable. It noted the testimony of the Director-Secretary of SHA that "actual segregation is essential to the success of a program of public housing in Savannah." Noting this, it then proceeded to rule that, "If the people involved think that such is the case and if Negroes and whites desire to maintain voluntary segregation for their common good, there is certainly no law to prevent such cooperation. Neither the Fifth nor the Fourteenth Amendments operates positively to command integration of the races, but only negatively to forbid governmentally enforced segregation" (at 78).

But *governmentally* enforced racial segregation was conclusively alleged and proved here, not "voluntary" segregation. Because of this, the court below was bound to enjoin the segregation. Such an injunction is required by application to this case of principles firmly established by this Court in *Bolling* v. *Sharpe*, 347 U. S. 497; *Buchanan* v. *Warley, supra; Shelley* v. *Kraemer, supra; Hurd* v. *Hodge, supra* and *Barrows* v. *Jackson, supra.*

CONCLUSION

For the foregoing reasons, petitioner prays that a writ of certiorari issue to review the judgment of the court below.

Respectfully submitted,

THURGOOD MARSHALL
10 Columbus Circle
New York 19, N. Y.

CONSTANCE BAKER MOTLEY
10 Columbus Circle
New York 19, N. Y.

A. T. WALDEN
28 Butler Street, N. E.
Atlanta 3, Georgia

Attorneys for Petitioner

INDEX TO APPENDIX

APPENDIX A

Opinion of Court of Appeals, Fifth Circuit

In the

UNITED STATES COURT OF APPEALS

For the Fifth Circuit

No. 16866

Queen Cohen,

Appellant,

versus

Public Housing Administration, *et al.,*

Appellees.

APPEAL FROM THE UNITED STATES DISTRICT COURT FOR THE
SOUTHERN DISTRICT OF GEORGIA.

(June 30, 1958.)

Before:

Rives, Brown and Wisdom,

Circuit Judges.

Rives, *Circuit Judge*:

The complaint was originally brought by eighteen Negro residents of Savannah, Georgia for an injunction, declaratory judgment and money damages on account of racial segregation in public housing in that City, allegedly enforced by the Public Housing Administration (hereinafter called P.H.A.) and the Housing Authority of Savannah (hereinafter called S.H.A.). Earlier orders of the district court dismissing the action[1] were affirmed in part and reversed in part and remanded.[2]

After remand, but prior to the commencement of trial, seventeen parties plaintiff voluntarily withdrew,[3] leaving the appellant, Queen Cohen, as the sole plaintiff. At the conclusion of the trial, the district court found as a fact, inter alia, that "Queen Cohen never made an application for admission in the Fred Wessels Homes or any other public housing project in Savannah."

The appellant's first specification of error is that:

> "The trial court erred in dismissing appellant's suit, after a full trial on the merits, on the ground that appellant failed to prove that she had ever made application for admission to Fred Wessels Homes."

The complaint alleged that: "Each of the plaintiffs has been denied admission to Fred Wessels Homes solely because of race and color." In their answer, the defendants denied "that these defendants have determined upon and presently enforce an administrative policy of racial segregation in public housing in the City of Savannah, Georgia," and denied the allegation that "Each of the plaintiffs has been denied admission to Fred Wessels Homes solely be-

---

[1] Heyward v. Public Housing Administration, S. D. Ga. 1955, 135 F. Supp. 217.

[2] Heyward v. Public Housing Administration, 5th Cir. 1956, 238 F. 2d 689.

[3] Mr. Stillwell, Secretary and Executive Director of S.H.A., testified upon the trial that none of those seventeen had ever applied for admission to Fred Wessels Homes; that fifteen of them had applied for and been admitted to another project, Fellwood Homes; and that two had never applied for any kind of housing.

cause of race or color." The evidence showed that P.H.A. was operating under its regulation quoted in full in our former opinion,[4] which requires that:

> "Programs for the development of low-rent housing, in order to be eligible for PHA assistance, must reflect equitable provisions for eligible families of all races determined on the approximate volume of their respective needs for such housing." (PHA Housing Manual, Section 102.1)

Its policies and practices were more fully described in the testimony of Mr. Silverman, its Assistant Commissioner for Management, quoted in the margin.[5]

---

[4] Heyward v. Public Housing Administration, 5th Cir. 1956, 238 F. 2d 689, at p. 697.

[5] "Q. Now, what are the policies and practices of the Public Housing Administration with respect to racial occupancy of low-rent housing projects?

"A. It is the policy of the Public Housing Administration to assure that equitable treatment is afforded to all eligible families in a locality, and that all eligible families who are admitted to housing projects by housing authorities are treated equally with respect to income limits or rents to be charged and other conditions of occupanys (sic).

"Q. What is the policy and position of the Public Housing Administration with respect to low-rent housing projects in Savannah or elsewhere as to whether or not they are operated by the Local Authority on a segregated or non-segregated basis?

"A. We have not required Housing Authorities to either segregate or non-segregate in housing projects. We have required that the housing program in every locality be available to all segments of the eligible low income families in that locality. We have not prescribed the precise fashion in which the Housing Authority shall extend that equality of treatment to the residents of the locality.

"Q. Is that policy based on your interpretation of the requirements and policies of the Housing Act itself?

"A. Yes. It is based upon our construction of the United States Housing Act and particularly the 1949 Housing Act Amendment. The very act which created the preferences that have been discussed here, the preferences extended to displaced families, when it was being considered in the Congress, in the Senate, a motion was made to attach a non-segregated requirement to the statute.

The Housing Authority of Savannah operated, or had under construction, 2170 dwelling units of which 1120 were designated for negro occupancy and 1050 for white. The project known as Fred Wessels Homes was intended for white occupancy, but Mr. Stillwell, the Secretary and Executive Director of S.H.A., denied in his testimony that negroes had ever been refused admission to that project.⁶ At the

---

That was defeated. It is our view that that action was Congressional recognition of the fact that local practices vary in the United States, and that some Local Authorities did maintain separate projects by race and other integrated, but the failure to enact a specific congressional prohibition against it was recognition that a variety of practices might prevail.

"Q. With respect to the low-rent housing program throughout the country, that is, those projects to which PHA gives financial assistance to what extent has there been integrated occupancy as to those projects?

"A. As of December 31st, last, which is the last statistical tabulation we have, on 445 projects, approximately, containing some 168,000 dwelling units, representing about 43 percent of the entire program, were operated on an integrated basis.

"Q. Would there be any objection on the part of the Public Housing Administration if the Savannah Housing Authority, or any other Local Authority, were to determine to operate a low-rent housing project on integrated basis?

"A. None whatsoever."

On cross-examination, Mr. Silverman testified:

"Q. Now, I believe you stated that your Agency interpreted the defeat of the anti-discrimination with respect to the Public Housing bill as an authorization from Congress that you and your Agency might approve segregation or integration in any particular Local Authority, or any particular locality that a Housing Authority might want to practice in public housing. Is that right?

"A. Mrs. Motley, I don't mean to quibble with you, but we didn't recognize it as that kind of an authorization. We recognized it as Congressional recognition of the fact that practices varied among the various localities in the country with respect to the low-rent housing."

⁶ "Q. Well, were you taking applications from negroes for the Fred Wessels Homes at anytime?

"A. For occupancy in there?

"Q. Yes.

"A. No. I have never been asked to do so. We have never had an application from a negro for occupancy in any white project

same time, Mr. Stillwell candidly admitted that his hope for success of a program of public housing for people unable to pay the cost of decent and adequate private housing lay in the maintenance of actual segregation.[7]

---

and by the same token we have never had an application from a white man to go into a negro project. We have never had that to come up.

"Q. If a negro applied for admission to the Fred Wessels Homes would you put him in there? Is that what you are saying?

"A. No. He would be given consideration, but I don't know what I would do.

"Q. You wouldn't put him in there, would you?

"A. I don't know what I would do. I have never had the question to come up.

"Q. You know that this case is concerning your refusal to admit negroes to the Fred Wessels Homes?

"A. Yes, but we have never refused to take them in there."

[7] "A. Well, as you know, our white projects are predominately (sic) occupied by what is generally known as 'Georgia Crackers', and you know that he would never consent to occupy a home adjacent to or mixed up with the colored families. Consequently, it would mean that the white projects would eventually be overwhelmingly negro, if not a 100 percent negro, and the average income of the negro is less than the average income of the white population of that same caliber, and consequently the average rent per unit would be much less and it is a question in my mind whether the rents would maintain the property and pay off its debts.

"Q. In other words, do I understand you to say that if colored people were allowed to come into the white units the white people would move out?

"A. That's right.

"Q. And there would not be sufficient eligible colored people to occupy the units sufficient to pay the amount due on the debt of that particular property. Is that right?

"A. Yes, and when I say that I mean sufficient eligible of the higher groups of rents. We have to have a certain percentage of tenants who pay a minimum rent of $15.00 and graduate on up so as to average down to enough to meet the expenses plus the subsistive to retire the principal and interest on the notes and bonds as they mature, and with this lessened income I question whether there would be enough to meet all the obligations.

"Q. And there could be a default, in your payments?

"A. Yes, that's right, the bonds, and another thing it would break down the racial equity.

The appellant did not claim that she had filed any written application. Her testimony was that she went to make her application "around 1952, during the time I had to move," that the building of the Fred Wessels Homes had then been completed, but "It was empty and I didn't know who was going to take it, white or colored, and so I went to apply for one." She testified that she went to the office of the Fred Wessels Project.[8] Mr. Stillwell, the Secretary and Executive Director of S.H.A., and Millard Williams, an employee of S.H.A. from 1951 to 1955, were brought into the courtroom for purposes of identification. The appellant was unable to identify either of them as the one with whom she had talked.[9]

Appellant testified that her cousin, Susie Parker, had accompanied her when she went to make her application. When Susie Parker came to testify, she positively identified Millard Williams as the one with whom the conversation took place.

In rebuttal, both Stillwell and Williams denied having had any such conversation, or ever having seen the appellant

---

"Q. Explain what you mean by breaking down the racial equity?

"A. Well, that's the point that Miss Motley has been trying to bring out, that if it was turned into all colored then the white eligible tenants would be deprived of their occupancy of the white projects and we would default in our contract with the PHA because we did not maintain a racial equity."

[8] "When I went into the office I met a clerk boy, and so I told him that I wanted to apply for a house there. He took me upstairs. When I got upstairs he showed me a room and in that room were two white ladies, and so I asked them could I put in for a house there. She took me to another office where there was a white man sitting there. The white woman told me to explain it to this man, and so I explained to him, I said, 'I came to put in for a house.' He said, 'Negroes are not allowed here. Go to Fellwood.' That was his remarks to me and so I turned around and walked out."

[9] "Q. It was this man here? Is that him?

"A. I wouldn't say, but he was a slender built man. I only saw him once and then for about three minutes."

or her cousin prior to the trial. Mr. Stillwell testified further that the Fred Wessels Homes had not even been built in 1952, that there were then no buildings on the site.

Stillwell and Williams denied that there had been any application or attempt to apply for admission to Fred Wessels Homes specifically on the part of any one of the eighteen original plaintiffs, and generally on the part of any other negro. None of the seventeen other original plaintiffs testified in rebuttal, nor was any reason given for their failure to testify.

The district court had the advantage of seeing and hearing the witnesses, while this Court may only read their testimony. Upon the present record, it is an understatement to say that the pertinent fact-finding by the district court does not appear to be clearly erroneous Rule 52(a), Federal Rules of Civil Procedure.

That, however, is not the end of this case, for appellant next contends that she was not required to prove that she applied for or was denied such admission because equity does not require the doing of a vain act. Appellant argues that similar acts have been held to be vain in cases involving governmentally enforced racial segregation, citing *School Board of City of Charlottesville, Va.* v. *Allen,* 4th Cir. 1956, 240 F. 2d. 59, and *Gibson* v. *Board of Public Instruction of Dade County,* 5th Cir. 1957, 246 F. 2d. 913.

School Board of City of Charlottesville, Va. v. *Allen, supra,* involved actions in behalf of Negro school children to enjoin School Boards from enforcing racial segregation. Applications had been made to the Boards to take action toward abolishing the requirement of segregation in the schools, and no action had been taken. The Boards contended that, before the plaintiffs would be entitled to injunctive relief, they must have individually applied for and been denied admission to a particular school. The Fourth Circuit, speaking through the late Chief Judge Parker, said:

" * * * The answer is that in view of the announced policy of the respective school boards any such application to a school other than a segregated school maintained for Colored people would have been futile; and equity does not require the doing of a vain thing as a condition of relief."

School Board of City of Charlottesville, Va. v. *Allen, supra,* 240 F. 2d. at pp. 63, 64.

The situation was almost identical in *Gibson* v. *Board of Public Instruction of Dade County, supra.* The plaintiffs had petitioned the Board of Public Instruction to abolish racial segregation in the public schools as soon as practicable, and the Board had refused. Relying upon and quoting from Chief Judge Parker's opinion in the *City of Charlottesville Case, supra,* this Court held that: "Under the circumstances alleged, it was not necessary for the plaintiffs to make application for admission to a particular school." 246 F. 2d. at p. 914.

At least two material distinctions exist between those cases and the present case: First, in each of those cases the plaintiffs had placed themselves on record as desiring practically the same relief as that sought from the court. Here, in the absence of any attempt to apply for admission to the Fred Wessels Homes, there is no reasonably certain proof that the appellant actually desired in some earlier year, say 1952, to become a tenant in that public housing. Testimony, years after the critical event, as to what one's intentions were cannot take the place of acts done at that time. Secondly, in each of the cases relied on, it was admitted that discriminatory segregation of the races was being enforced by the defendant Board, while, as has already been indicated, in the present case, in both the pleadings and the proof, governmentally enforced segregation is denied.

In her reply brief, the appellant cites a third case in support of her contention that she was not required to prove that she applied for or was denied admission to the public housing project, *Staub* v. *City of Baxley*, 1958, 355 U. S. 313. The pertinent holding in that case was thus expressed:

> "The first of the nonfederal grounds relied on by appellee, and upon which the decision of the Court of Appeals rests, is that appellant lacked standing to attack the constitutionality of the ordinance because she made no attempt to secure a permit under it. This is not an adequate nonfederal ground of decision. The decisions of this Court have uniformly held that the failure to apply for a license under an ordinance which on its face violates the Constitution does not preclude review in this Court of a judgment of conviction under such an ordinance. *Smith* v. *Cahoon*, 283 U. S. 553, 562; *Lovell* v. *Griffin*, 303 U. S. 444, 452. 'The Constitution can hardly be thought to deny one subjected to the restraints of such an ordinance the right to attack its constitutionality, because he has not yielded to its demands.' *Jones* v. *Opelika*, 316 U. S. 584, 602, dissenting opinion, adopted *per curiam* on rehearing, 319 U. S. 103, 104."

Staub v. *City of Baxley*, *supra*, 355 U. S. at p. 319.

Clearly, that decision is not applicable here, for in that case the appellant had a legal right to engage in the occupation regardless of the ordinance, while here a tenant could not be admitted to a housing project without having made an application. No one could reasonably contend that by applying for admission to a public housing project the appellant would be yielding to any unconstitutional demand.

We conclude that the appellant-plaintiff has no standing to maintain this action when she has not been denied admission to a public housing project on account of her race or color. That is the very gist of her claim. Absent such standing, there is no justiciable claim or controversy.[10]

Mr. Stillwell's testimony has been noted (footnote 7, *supra*) to the effect that in his opinion actual segregation is essential to the success of a program of public housing in Savannah. If the people involved think that such is the case and if Negroes and whites desire to maintain voluntary segregation for their common good, there is certainly no law to prevent such cooperation. Neither the Fifth nor the Fourteenth Amendment operates positively to command integration of the races but only negatively to forbid governmentally enforced segregation.[11]

The judgment of dismissal is

AFFIRMED.

---

[10] Associated Industries v. Ickes, 2nd Cir. 1943, 134 F. 2d 694, 700.

[11] Cf. Avery v. Wichita Falls Independent School District, 5th Cir. 1957, 241 F. 2d 230, 233; Rippy v. Borders, 5th Cir. 1957, 250 F. 2d 690, 692.

Judgment of Court of Appeals

Extract from the Minutes of June 30, 1958

No. 16,866

QUEEN COHEN,

versus

PUBLIC HOUSING ADMINISTRATION, *et al.*

This cause came on to be heard on the transcript of the record from the United States District Court for the Southern District of Georgia, and was argued by counsel;

On consideration whereof, It is now here ordered and adjudged by this Court that the judgment of the said District Court in this cause be, and the same is hereby, affirmed;

It is further ordered and adjudged that the appellant, Queen Cohen, be condemned to pay the Costs of this cause in this Court for which execution may be issued out of the said District Court.

Order Denying Rehearing

Extract from the Minutes of August 11, 1958

No. 16,866

QUEEN COHEN,

versus

PUBLIC HOUSING ADMINISTRATION, *et al.*

It is ordered by the Court that the petition for rehearing filed in this cause be, and the same is hereby, denied.

APPENDIX B

Regulations, Statutes And Constitutional Provisions Involved

HHFA
PHA
2-21-51   Low-Rent Housing Manual   102.1

Racial Policy

The following general statement of racial policy shall be applicable to all low-rent housing projects developed and operated under the United States Housing Act of 1937, as amended:

1. Programs for the development of low-rent housing, in order to be eligible for PHA assistance, must reflect equitable provision for eligible families of all races determined on the approximate volume and urgency of their respective needs for such housing.

2. While the selection of tenants and the assigning of dwelling units are primarily matters for local determination, urgency of need and the preferences prescribed in the Housing Act of 1949 are the basic statutory standards for the selection of tenants.

Title 42, United States Code, §1402:

(1) Low-rent housing. The term 'low-rent housing' means decent, safe, and sanitary dwellings within the financial reach of families of low income, and developed and administered to promote serviceability, efficiency, economy, and stability, and embraces all necessary appurtenances thereto. The dwellings in low-rent housing as defined in this Act [§1401 et seq. of this title] shall be available solely for families whose net annual income at the time of admission, less exemption of $100

for each minor member of the family other than the head of the family and his spouse, does not exceed five times the annual rental (including the value or cost to them of water, electricity, gas, other heating and cooking fuels, and other utilities) of the dwellings to be furnished such families. For the sole purpose of determining eligibility for continued occupancy, a public housing agency may allow, from the net income of any family, an exemption for each minor member of the family (other than the head of the family and his spouse) of either (a) $100, or (b) all or any part of the annual income of such minor. For the purposes of this subsection, a minor shall mean a person less than 21 years of age.

(14) Veteran. The term 'veteran' shall mean a person who has served in the active military or naval service of the United States at any time (i) on or after September 16, 1940, and prior to July 26, 1947, (ii) on or after April 6, 1917, and prior to November 11, 1918, or (iii) on or after June 27, 1950, and prior to such date thereafter as shall be determined by the President, and who shall have been discharged or released therefrom under conditions other than dishonorable. The term 'serviceman' shall mean a person in the active military or naval service of the United States who has served therein at any time (i) on or after September 16, 1940, and prior to July 26, 1947, (ii) on or after April 6, 1917, and prior to November 11, 1918, or (iii) on or after June 27, 1950, and prior to such date thereafter as shall be determined by the President.

Title 42, United States Code, §1410(g):

(g) Veterans' preference. Every contract made pursuant to this Act [§1401 et seq. of this title] for annual contributions for any low-rent housing project shall require that the public housing agency, as among low-income families which are eligible applicants for occupancy in dwellings of given sizes and at specified rents, shall extend the following preferences in the selection of tenants:

First, to families which are to be displaced by any low-rent housing project or by any public slum-clearance, redevelopment or urban renewal project, or through action of a public body or court, either through the enforcement of housing standards or through the demolition, closing, or improvement of dwelling units, or which were so displaced within three years prior to making application to such public housing agency for admission to any low-rent housing: Provided, That as among such projects or actions the public housing agency may from time to time extend a prior preference or preferences: And Provided further, That, as among families within any such preference group such families first preference shall be given to families of disabled veterans whose disability has been determined by the Veterans' Administration to be service-connected, and second preference shall be given to families of deceased veterans and servicemen whose death has been determined by the Veterans' Administration to be service-connected, and third preference shall be given to families of other veterans and servicemen;

Second, to families of other veterans and servicemen and as among such families first preference shall be given to families of disabled veterans whose disability has been determined by the Veterans' Administration to be service-connected, and second preference shall be given to families of deceased veterans and servicemen whose death has been determined by the Veterans' Administration to be service-connected.

Title 42, United States Code, §1415:

(8) Every contract made pursuant to this Act [§1401 et seq. of this title] for annual contributions for any low-rent housing project initiated after March 1, 1949, shall provide that—

(a) the public housing agency shall fix maximum income limits for the admission and for the continued occupancy of families in such housing, that such maximum income limits and all revisions thereof shall be subject to the prior approval of the Authority [Public Housing Administration], and that the Authority [Public Housing Administration] may require the public housing agency to review and to revise such maximum income limits if the Authority [Public Housing Administration] determines that changed conditions in the locality make such revisions necessary in achieving the purposes of this Act [§1401 et seq. of this title];

(b) a duly authorized official of the public housing agency involved shall make periodic written statements to the Authority [Public Housing Administration] that an investigation has been made of each family admitted to the low-rent housing project involved during the period covered thereby, and that, on the basis of the report of said investigation, he has found that each such family at the time of its admission (i) had a net family income not exceeding the maximum income limits theretofore fixed by the public housing agency (and approved by the Authority [Public Housing Administration]) for admission of families of low income to such housing; and (ii) lived in an unsafe, insanitary, or overcrowded dwelling, or was to be displaced by any low-rent housing project or by any public slum-clearance, redevelopment or urban renewal project, or through action of a public body or court, either through the enforcement of housing standards or through the demolition, closing or improvement of a dwelling unit or units, or actually was without housing, or was about to be without housing as a result of a court order of eviction, due to causes other than the fault of the tenant: Provided, That the requirement in (ii) shall not be applicable in the case of the family of any veteran or serviceman (or of any deceased veteran or serviceman) where application for admission to such housing is made not later than March 1, 1959.

(c) in the selection of tenants (i) the public housing agency shall not discriminate against families, otherwise eligible for admission to such housing, because their incomes are derived in whole or in part from public assistance and (ii) in initially selecting families for admission to dwellings of given sizes and at specified rents the public housing agency shall (subject to the preferences prescribed in subsection 10 (g) of this Act [§1410(g) of this title]) give preference to families having the most urgent housing needs, and thereafter, in selecting families for admission to such dwellings, shall give due consideration the urgency of the families' housing needs; and . . .

Title 42, United States Code, §1982:

1982. Property rights of citizens.—All citizens of the United States shall have the same right, in every State and Territory, as is enjoyed by white citizens thereof to inherit, purchase, lease, sell, hold, and convey real and personal property.

Title 42, United States Code, §1983:

1983. Civil action for deprivation of rights.—Every person who, under color of any statute, ordinance, regulation, custom or usage, of any State or Territory, subjects, or causes to be subjected, any citizen of the United States or other person within the jurisdiction thereof to the deprivation of any rights, privileges, or immunities secured by the Constitution and laws, shall be liable to the party injured in an action at law, suit in equity, or other proper proceeding for redress.

Constitution of the United States:

Amendment 5—Due Process Clause

"No person shall be . . . deprived of life, liberty, or property, without due process of law . . . "

Amendment 14, §1—Due Process and Equal Protection Clauses:

" * * * nor shall any State deprive any person of life, liberty, or property, without due process of law; nor deny to any person within its jurisdiction the equal protection of the laws."

APPENDIX C

Opinion of United States District Court, District of Columbia, Filed May 8, 1953

IN THE

UNITED STATES DISTRICT COURT

FOR THE DISTRICT OF COLUMBIA

Civil Action No. 3991—52

(Filed May 8, 1953)

HEYWARD, *et al.*,

Plaintiffs,

—v.—

HOUSING AND HOME FINANCE AGENCY, *et al.*,

Defendants.

The Court: This is an action to restrain the Commissioner of the Public Housing Administration from advancing any funds under the United States Housing Act of 1937, as amended, and otherwise participating, in the construction and operation of certain housing projects in the City of Savannah, Georgia.

These projects are being constructed and will be operated by local authorities with the aid of Federal Funds.

The basis of the action is that it has been officially announced that the project referred to in the complaint will be open only to white residents. The plaintiffs are people of the colored race who contend that such a limitation is a violation of their Constitutional rights.

The Court has grave doubt whether this action lies in the light of the doctrine enunciated in the case of *Massachusetts* v. *Mellon*, 262 U. S. 447, but assuming, arguendo, that the action may be maintained, the Court is of the opinion that no violation of law or Constitutional rights on the part of the defendants has been shown.

It appears from the affidavit submitted in support of the defendants' motion for a summary judgment that there are several projects that have been or are being constructed in the City of Savannah under the Housing Act, some of which are limited to white residents and others to colored residents, and that a greater number of accommodations has been set aside for colored residents. In other words, we have no situation here where colored people are being deprived of opportunities or accommodations furnished by the Federal Government that are accorded to people of the white rice. Accommodations are being accorded to people of both races.

Under the so-called "separate but equal" doctrine, which is still the law under the Supreme Court decisions, it is entirely proper and does not constitute a violation of Constitutional rights for the Federal Government to require people of the white and colored races to use separate facilities, provided equal facilities are furnished to each.

There is another aspect of this matter which the Court considers of importance. The Congress has conferred discretionary authority on the administrative agency to determine for what projects Federal funds shall be used. There are very few limitations in the statute on the power of the administrator, and there is no limitation as to racial segregation.

The Congress has a right to appropriate money for such purposes as it chooses under the General Welfare clause of Article I, Section 8, of the Constitution. It has a right to appropriate money for purpose "A" but not for purpose "B," so long as purpose "A" is a public purpose.

Under the circumstances, the Court is of the opinion that the plaintiffs have no cause of action and the defendants' motion for summary judgment is granted.

(Thereupon, the above entitled matter was concluded.)

ALEXANDER HOLTZOFF,
District Judge.

IN THE

Supreme Court of the United States

October Term, 1958

No. 505

———————•———————

QUEEN COHEN

Petitioner,

versus

PUBLIC HOUSING ADMINISTRATION AND
HOUSING AUTHORITY OF SAVANNAH,

Respondents.

BRIEF ON BEHALF OF RESPONDENT, HOUSING AUTHORITY OF SAVANNAH IN OPPOSITION TO PETITION FOR WRIT OF CERTIORARI TO THE UNITED STATES COURT OF APPEALS FOR THE FIFTH DISTRICT

SHELBY MYRICK, SR.
P. O. Box 24
Savannah, Georgia

GEORGE C. HEYWARD
East Broad and Oglethorpe Ave.
Savannah, Ga.

*Attorneys for Respondent,
Housing Authority of Savannah*

TABLE OF CASES

IN THE

Supreme Court of the United States

October Term, 1958

QUEEN COHEN,

Petitioner

versus

No. 505

PUBLIC HOUSING ADMIN-
ISTRATION and HOUSING
AUTHORITY OF SAVANNAH,

Respondents

BRIEF ON BEHALF OF RESPONDENT, HOUSING AUTHORITY OF SAVANNAH AND ITS OFFICERS

I

The Respondents, HOUSING AUTHORITY OF SAVANNAH and its officers, of the Respondents in the above stated case, respectfully file this Brief in opposition to the Petition or Motion of QUEEN COHEN praying for the grant of the Writ of Certiorari in this case directed to the United States Court of Appeals for the Fifth Circuit by the Honorable Supreme Court of the United States.

The Fifth Circuit Court of Appeals in the decision set forth in the Brief of the attorneys for Queen Cohen upheld the decision of the District Court of the United

States for the Southern District of Georgia in dismissing Queen Cohen's case upon the grounds:

(1) That she had not applied for admission into the Fred Wessels Project;

(2) That she had no preference to be admitted because she was not a displaced person, and, what was probably an orbiter dicta statement in the opinion of the Fifth Circuit, that Court held that there could be voluntary segregation of the races in Public Housing Projects.

It is earnestly submitted by these Respondents that the case presented is not one of primary importance in any particular, as counsel for Petitioner endeavors to set forth.

As appears in the record of the proceedings in the District Court and also in brief of Petitioner, as we will more particularly point out later in this Brief, there were originally eighteen plaintiffs, seventeen of whom the record shows were displaced persons, QUEEN COHEN WAS NOT A DISPLACED PERSON. The case was pending in the District Court for several years, having been once dismissed on motion without any evidence being submitted, and when no plaintiffs appeared or testified, and later tried on its merits after the Fifth Circuit had ordered a trial and reversed the District Court in dismissing the case on motion. The record shows that when the case was ordered to trial in the District Court in Savannah counsel for the plaintiffs arose and moved to strike seventeen of the plaintiffs, stating that he had only just learned the day before that these plaintiffs would not proceed. We will elaborate upon this later in this

Brief. This left one sole plaintiff, Queen Cohen. Her case is of no paramount importance as we will show, and no principles of paramount importance are involved in her case warranting a Writ of Certiorari to be granted by this Honorable Court.

While the attorneys of the Department of Justice for the Public Housing Administration will fully set forth the position of the Public Housing Administration with reference to this petition for certiorari, we cannot refrain from calling attention in this Brief to the attitude of the Public Housing Administration with reference to the proceedings in this case. We do this because we feel that the defenses of the Public Housing Administration and the Housing Authority of Savannah are almost inseparably intertwined. We called attention to this fact in our Brief in this case before the Circuit Court of Appeals of the Fifth Circuit, and here we are repeating substantially what was in our Brief before the Circuit Court of Appeals of the Fifth Circuit.

It is submitted by counsel for Respondents that as held in the District of Columbia case, the opinion of which is attached to the brief of counsel for Petitioner, the Public Housing Administration of the United States, as the administrative agency, has the discretion as to what project federal funds shall be granted and for what purpose used. (See page 40 of the Brief of Petitioner.) Accordingly, we submit that the Public Housing Administration had a perfect right to grant and allot funds for the building of the Fred Wessels Project, a white unit, as well as to grant funds for the building of another colored project in Savannah, particularly new units for colored people immediately adjacent to the Fred Wessels Tract.

It is perfectly legal for the Public Housing Administration to grant money for the building of white and colored projects, and it establishes no policy as to admitting and not admitting colored people into the white project and admitting and not admitting white people into the colored project. After one of these projects for white people is finished and ready for occupancy, then it seems that under certain circumstances in the light of the decisions of this Honorable Court a colored person might have a right to apply for admission and be admitted, provided such colored person files a proper application and brings himself within the eligible class to live in a low-cost housing project. This case does not raise any such question. This record shows that the District Court under a conflict of evidence held that Queen Cohen had never applied for admission into the Fred Wessels Project and that furthermore she had no preference and that she was not a displaced person. The question was decided without the intervention of a jury and the District Judge had a right to decide the conflict of evidence, and he did so, and the Fifth Circuit upheld that finding of the District Judge.

In order for any person, white or colored, to be eligible for a low-cost housing project, such person must necessarily file a written application with the proper authority so that the qualifications of such person may be determined. There are various qualifications which must be considered of any such person applying, such as the earnings of the person, his present housing condition, composition of family, what his status is as a citizen, whether a communist or not, and whether otherwise fit to be an occupant of such project. Furthermore, such applicant even if he applies for admission in the proper way and is otherwise qualified such person can have no preference under the statute unless such persons falls within the class designated as a displaced person or a veteran or some other qualified status.

Petitioner is endeavoring very adroitly to have this Court grant the writ of certiorari upon the theory that this Plaintiff has a right to enjoin the policy of the Housing Authority of Savannah of having separate projects for white and separate projects for colored, and also enjoin the Public Housing Administration from granting funds for such purposes. Before any such contention could be made, there must be a qualified and eligible plaintiff who would be entitled to admission in a white project. Merely to bring forth some unqualified colored person and ask for an injunction against the Housing Authority of Savannah to abandon its policy of having separate units for white and colored, WHICH IN FACT ALREADY EXISTS AT THIS TIME, would in no way be legally sufficient. Besides, as is shown in this record, neither the Public Housing Administration nor the Housing Authority of Savannah have ever fixed any policy of denying colored people to a white unit.

It is earnestly submitted that for any colored person to bring such an action such person must make application to be admitted into a white project and show that such person is qualified under the law to be admitted, and therefore have the right to maintain such an action as Petitioner says she is trying to institute and have established in her brief.

If the policy of the Public Housing Administration and the Housing Authority of Savannah of establishing separate projects is legally wrong, then proper cases should have been brought originally before the money was granted for these projects and before the projects were constructed. The Petitioner undertook to do this in the District of Columbia and failed and never thereafter instituted a similar suit.

II

Counsel for Queen Cohen contend that it is not necessary for the Plaintiff in this case to have applied for admission into the Fred Wessels Project and endeavor to uphold their contention by citing the two cases set forth in their brief, to-wit: **School Board of City of Charlottesville, V. vs. Allen, 240 F. 2d, 59; and Gibson v. Board of Public Instruction of Dade County, 246 F. 2d, 913,** which were the basis of a portion of the opinion of the Fifth Circuit Court of Appeals.

It may here be noted that if Petitioner's counsel felt that they did not have to prove that their client, Queen Cohen, applied for admission, then may we inquire why all the strenuous effort made to bolster their case from lengthy testimony of Queen Cohen and her cousin tending to show that application had been made by Queen Cohen to be admitted to the Fred Wessels Project and had been denied. As a matter of fact, the District Judge held that Queen Cohen and her witness perjured themselves, and this fact should have been perfectly apparent to Queen Cohen's counsel under the evidence in the record.

It doesn't follow legally at all that because there was a policy in Savannah, adopted by the Housing Authority in Savannah, of maintaining separate units under the grant of funds for erection of such projects by the Public Housing Administration, that colored people would be denied admission into a white project. On Page 127 of the record, Mr. Stillwell, Executive Director of the Housing Authority of Savannah testified that he had never considered the question as to what would be done if some Negro actually applied for admission into a white project inasmuch as the Housing Authority of Savannah had no fixed or established policy of admitting Negroes into white housing units or not admitting them. Furthermore, Mr. Silverman, Assistant Commissioner for Management of the Public Housing Administration testified on Page 168 of the record that the Public Housing Administration had made no requirement as to either segregation or non-segregation in housing projects, and the Public Housing Administration had never prescribed the fashion in which equality of treatment should be required in any given locality.

As contended by Respondent's counsel before the Fifth Circuit Court of Appeals and as decided by that Court in the cases of the **Schoolboard of the City of Charlottesville vs. Allen, 240 F. 2d,63, and Gibson vs. Board of Public Instruction, 246 F. 2d,914,** a clearly defined policy had been previously publicly announced by each School Board that no colored person would be admitted into a white school. Under such public announcement, the Fourth Circuit and Fifth Circuit held that it would be useless for any colored person to formally apply for admission into the white schools in either of those localities, all of the requirements of the respective School Boards as to admission having been complied with but admission denied on account of race. The Petitioner in her brief on the Writ of Certiorari on pages 13, 14, 15, 16, 17 and 18, and particularly on page 18 endeavors to contend that the Fifth Circuit in the present case of Queen Cohen made invalid distinctions between the Charlottesville case and the Dade County case. The Fifth Circuit did no such thing.

In these cases the Plaintiffs alleged and proved that previous to the filing of their complaints they had made known to the respective School Board their desire to attend white schools, and had been told that a fixed policy of racial segregation had been adopted and they would not be admitted. For the present case, there was no application by Queen Cohen to any one and the first notice to the Housing Authority of her desire to occupy a unit in a housing project came to the Housing Authority when it was served with a copy of the petition.

In connection with this woman Queen Cohen being the only Plaintiff in this case and not an eligible party under the statute, it is pertinent to point out that she was a married woman, had a husband with whom she was living, that she did not work herself, and set herself up as a housewife and the mother of four children. (See Pages 133 and 206 of the record). It is significant from both a factual and legal standpoint that the husband's name does not appear as a party plaintiff, nor did this woman testify that she had her husband's consent to appear as a party plaintiff and to testify that she desired to live in Fred Wessels' Homes, his name in this respect never being mentioned by her. Under Section 53-501 of the Code of Georgia, the husband is the head of the family and the wife is subject to him.

Her legal existence is merged in the husband. She has no income herself and therefore could not have qualified for admission, and has no legal standing in this proceeding.

The Supreme Court of Georgia in the case of **Pace v. Pace, 154 Ga., Page 712** has held that the husband has the right to fix the matrimonial residence without the consent of the wife, and she is bound to follow the husband. But our Supreme Court has never held that a wife has the right to fix the matrimonial residence without the consent of the husband and that he is bound to follow her. Let it be noted that among the names formerly appearing as parties plaintiffs in this case are the names of several husbands and wives together.

So that we assert, that regardless of whether Queen Cohen ever properly or actually applied for admission into Fred Wessels' Homes or was a displaced person with a preference, she was not a legal party to this suit and had and has no legal standing as a party plaintiff in Court.

She was brought forward by Atlanta, Georgia, counsel for the NAACP and counsel from the New York Headquarters of this organization, as a last resort in a hopeless case to endeavor to bolster a case in which there was and is no merit and for which there was no excuse whatsoever for filing and maintaining in the Court below or for appealing to this Court for relief.

The petition of plaintiffs in this case, Section 21, (Page 14 of the record) alleges that at the time the Fred Wessels Homes were ready for occupancy all the Plaintiffs (including, of course, Queen Cohen) had a preference for admission to the Fred Wessels Homes by virtue of the fact that they had been displaced from the site of this project, or will be displaced from the site of another public housing project to be built adjacent to the Fred Wessels Homes. As a matter of fact, however, all of these Plaintiffs other than Queen Cohen lived on the Fred Wessels' site and NOT IN THE NEW SITE ADJACENT TO THE FRED WESSELS HOMES. And it appears from the testimony of Mr. Stillwell (page 119 of the record) that in this new site a splendid set of homes, for Negroes, was in process of being erected adjacent to the Fred Wessels Homes. The foregoing is very pertinent because Queen Cohen testified (Page 139 of the record) that she had lived in that particular locality ("the bottom", she termed it) all her life and did not want to move out. She claimed as justification for wanting to live in the Fred Wessels Homes among white people only she "wanted to be comfortable." And yet as just pointed out splendid new homes for Negroes are built where Queen Cohen could apply for admission and be admitted and she would thus be housed in new, modern houses right in the neighborhood where she always had lived and certainly be "comfortable", more comfortable in fact than in the old houses where she now resides.

So that we repeat again, there is really no excuse or justification for this present litigation in behalf of ONLY ONE PERSON. This suit is now being appealed and pressed solely because the NAACP organization in New York is desirous of trying to establish a precedent in Georgia where there is no need or demand on the part of the Negroes in Savannah or in Georgia for any such proceeding.

The contention on the part of Petitioner's counsel that it would have been in vain for this Negro woman to have applied comes very late, and seems to have been entirely an afterthought, and apparently counsel are grasping at something to cause this Court to grant the petition for certiorari.

The main contention of the counsel for Queen Cohen in the Circuit Court of Appeals as appears from the record was that the defendants had refused to consider the Plaintiff for admission to certain housing projects which have been built in the City of Savannah, particularly a project called the Fred Wessels Homes, and that the Plaintiff, Queen Cohen, as a former resident of that site was denied the right to even make application for occupancy solely because of her race and color. It appears now in the petition for certiorari, counsel for the Petitioner have changed their tactics and contentions and are asking this Court to grant the writ of certiorari because they say that the Court below should have granted an injunction restraining the Defendants from having separate units for white and colored, and also from not admitting this woman, and this regardless of whether or not the Plaintiff, Queen Cohen, ever made application for admission to the white project known as Fred Wessels Homes.

Furthermore, we find nothing in the testimony of either Mr. Arthur Hanson of the Public Housing Administration in Atlanta, or in the testimony of Mr. Abner D. Silverman, an official of the Public Housing Administration in Washington, to warrant even an inference that the Public Housing Administration had instructed the Savannah Housing Authority to refuse to admit a Negro into a white project upon proper application being made and filed. We have previously in this brief quoted Mr. Stillwell's evidence to the effect that Negroes were permitted to apply at Fred Wessels Homes and that they were given application when they came in (R 95-96) and that he would give them an application if they came in, and that he had given three Negroes applications.

We consider now the two decisions cited in Petitioner's brief, to-wit: **School Board of City of Charlottsville, Va. v. Allen, 240 F 2d 59.** There it appeared that the respective school boards had announced a policy of segregated schools, that is, that no Negro would be admitted into a white school. The Court of Appeals accordingly held that it would have been futile for any Negro to have applied for admission in a white school. In the other case cited in the brief, to-wit: **Gibson v. Board of Public Instruction of Dade County, 246 F. 2d, 913,** which was an action for declaratory judgment, in the complaint which was dismissed by the District Judge, it appeared that the Negro plaintiffs in that case alleged that they had petitioned the Board of Public Instruction to abolish segregation in the public schools of the County as soon as practicable, and that the Board had refused and instead adhered to a statement of policy maintaining and conducting the schools on a non-integrated basis. It thus appears that these Negro Plaintiffs did in effect file applications for admission.

In the concluding portion of the Opinion of the Fifth Circuit Court of Appeals that Court referred to voluntary segregation as having happened in this case, with seventeen out of the eighteen former plaintiffs. As we interpret the language of the Circuit Court for the Fifth Circuit, that Court simply intended to hold that seventeen of these plaintiffs had voluntarily moved into a colored project after they were displaced on the site of the Fred Wessels Project and that they were so placed there by the Director of the Housing Authority of Savannah. That these seventeen plaintiffs, more or less, (some of them have disappeared entirely from Savannah) chose to be satisfied with their housing in the colored project prompted the Circuit Court to state the following:

> "If the people involved think that such is the case and if Negroes and whites desire to maintain voluntary segregation for their common good, there is certainly no law to prevent such cooperation. Neither the Fifth nor the Fourteenth Amendment operates positively to command integration of the races but only negatively to forbid governmentally enforced segregation."

As we have heretofore stated, this portion of the Opinion was probably orbiter dicta and is not a controlling part of the decision of the Fifth Circuit Court of Appeals.

RESPECTFULLY SUBMITTED,

Shelby Myrick Sr.
P. O. Box 24
Savannah, Georgia

George C. Heyward
East Broad and Oglethorpe Ave.
Savannah, Georgia

ATTORNEYS FOR RESPONDENT,
HOUSING AUTHORITY OF SAVANNAH

No. 505

In the Supreme Court of the United States

OCTOBER TERM, 1958

QUEEN COHEN, PETITIONER

v.

PUBLIC HOUSING ADMINISTRATION, ET AL.

ON PETITION FOR A WRIT OF CERTIORARI TO THE UNITED STATES COURT OF APPEALS FOR THE FIFTH CIRCUIT

BRIEF FOR THE RESPONDENT PUBLIC HOUSING ADMINISTRATION IN OPPOSITION

J. LEE RANKIN,
                    Solicitor General,
GEORGE COCHRAN DOUB,
            Assistant Attorney General,
ALAN S. ROSENTHAL,
SETH H. DUBIN,
                            Attorneys,
Department of Justice, Washington 25, D. C.

INDEX

CITATIONS

490378—58

In the Supreme Court of the United States

OCTOBER TERM, 1958

No. 505

QUEEN COHEN, PETITIONER

v.

PUBLIC HOUSING ADMINISTRATION, ET AL.

ON PETITION FOR A WRIT OF CERTIORARI TO THE UNITED STATES COURT OF APPEALS FOR THE FIFTH CIRCUIT

BRIEF FOR THE RESPONDENT PUBLIC HOUSING ADMINISTRATION IN OPPOSITION

OPINIONS BELOW

The opinion of the United States District Court for the Southern District of Georgia (R. 208–214) is reported *sub nom. Heyward, et al.* v. *Public Housing Administration, et al.*, at 154 F. Supp. 589. The opinion of the United States Court of Appeals for the Fifth Circuit (Pet. App. 21–30) is reported at 257 F. 2d 73. Earlier opinions in this litigation, *sub nom. Heyward, et al.* v. *Public Housing Administration, et al.*, are reported at 135 F. Supp. 217 and 238 F. 2d 689.

JURISDICTION

The judgment of the Court of Appeals was entered on June 30, 1958 (Pet. App. 31). A timely petition

(1)

for rehearing was denied on August 11, 1958 (Pet.
App. 32). The petition for a writ of certiorari was
filed on November 8, 1958. The jurisdiction of this
Court is invoked under 28 U. S. C. 1254 (1).

QUESTION PRESENTED

Whether the Public Housing Administration may
be enjoined from paying federal funds to a municipal
housing authority on the ground that public housing
projects owned and operated by the local authority
are maintained on a segregated basis, where both
courts below found that the petitioner never attempted
to apply for admission to any of those projects.

STATEMENT

This action was originally brought by eighteen Savannah residents who allegedly had been or would be
displaced from the site of a low-rent housing project
in Savannah known as "Fred Wessels Homes," which
is owned and operated by the respondent Savannah
Housing Authority (R. 1, 7, 8, 166–167). The complaint alleged that the Fred Wessels Homes were
maintained on a segregated basis and that each of the
plaintiffs had been denied admission to the project
solely because of race (R. 8). It was also alleged
that the Public Housing Administration, by financing
the Fred Wessels Homes, had violated the plaintiff's
rights under the Fifth and Fourteenth Amendments,
the Civil Rights Act (42 U. S. C. 1982), and the provisions of the United States Housing Act of 1937
(42 U. S. C. 1401–33), and of the Lanham Act (42
U. S. C. 1501–70) (R. 2–3, 7). The relief sought was
an injunction, declaratory judgment, and money damages (R. 3, 4, 16–19).

Before the trial of the action, all of the plaintiffs, except the petitioner Queen Cohen, voluntarily withdrew from the suit (R. 40). She conceded, at trial, that she had not filed written application for admission to the Fred Wessels Homes (R. 143). She testified, however, that "around 1952" she went to the project office, on the site of the project, to apply for an apartment, and was told by a man who was "sitting there" that "Negroes are not allowed here" (R. 131, 133). Although the petitioner was unable to identify the man to whom she spoke, her cousin, who testified that she accompanied the petitioner to the project office, identified the man as Millard Williams, a former manager of the Fred Wessels Homes, and the person to whom an application for admission to the project would have been made (R. 146, 151, 188, 189). For his part, Mr. Williams denied that he had ever seen the petitioner prior to the trial (R. 187–188). In addition, both he and W. H. Stillwell, Secretary and Executive Director of the Savannah Housing Authority, testified that, in 1952, there were no buildings on the Fred Wessels Homes site (R. 185, 189).

The District Court found that the petitioner "never made an application for admission in the Fred Wessels Homes or any other public housing project in Savannah" (R. 213). Accordingly, the court dismissed the action against the respondents (R. 215). The Court of Appeals affirmed. It held that "it is an understatement to say that" the District Court's finding that the petitioner never attempted to apply for admission "does not appear to be clearly erroneous * * *." (Pet. App. 27.) It further held that, in the absence of an application or at least an attempt to apply, the petitioner lacked standing to maintain the action (Pet. App. 27–30).

ARGUMENT

Without reaching the substance of the petitioner's contentions, it is clear that she lacks the standing necessary to maintain this action.

Both of the courts below have resolved against petitioner the factual question as to whether she attempted to apply for admission to the Fred Wessels Homes. A settled rule of this Court makes concurrent findings of two courts below final here in the absence of exceptional error. *Comstock* v. *Group of Investors*, 335 U. S. 211, 214; *Corn Products Co.* v. *Commissioner*, 350 U. S. 46, 51. Petitioner has failed to demonstrate that exceptional error was committed. To the contrary, the finding that petitioner did not attempt to apply for admission is fully supported by the testimony of the officials of the Savannah Housing Authority. (See *supra*, p. 3.)

The first manifestation by the petitioner that she wished to become a resident in the Fred Wessels Homes was the institution of this suit. We do not contend that the petitioner must have filed a formal application before she could have acquired a sufficient interest to maintain this suit. But, as the court below correctly held, since she had not even evinced a desire to gain residence in the Fred Wessels Homes, she could hardly complain that she was denied admission.

The only relief sought by the petitioner which is applicable to the Public Housing Administration is a declaration, together with an injunction, that the Public Housing Administration may not pay out federal funds to the Savannah Housing Authority for the construction, operation, and maintenance, by the Savannah Housing Authority, of a public housing project from which the petitioner, and other similarly situated Negroes, will be excluded solely because of their race. But petitioner clearly lacks standing to challenge the validity of the Public Housing Administration's disbursements. *Massachusetts* v. *Mellon,* 262 U. S. 447, 486–489; *Alabama Power Co.* v. *Ickes,* 302 U. S. 464, 478–479; *Doremus* v. *Board of Education,* 342 U. S. 429.[1]

CONCLUSION

It is respectfully submitted that the petition for a writ of certiorari should be denied.

J. LEE RANKIN,
Solicitor General.
GEORGE COCHRAN DOUB,
Assistant Attorney General.
ALAN S. ROSENTHAL,
SETH H. DUBIN,
Attorneys.

DECEMBER 1958.

---

[1] In their disposition of the case, the courts below did not have to consider other defenses, which were asserted by the Public Housing Administration, some of which we would urge are equally dispositive of the petitioner's complaint against that agency.

Lightning Source UK Ltd.
Milton Keynes UK
UKOW05f1810191217
314746UK00006B/611/P